THE STATES AND THEIR SYMBOLS

Mississippi
Facts and Symbols

by Karen Bush Gibson

Consultant:
Martin Hegwood
Senior Attorney
Office of the Mississippi Secretary of State

Hilltop Books

an imprint of Capstone Press
Mankato, Minnesota

Hilltop Books are published by Capstone Press
151 Good Counsel Drive, P.O. Box 669, Mankato, Minnesota 56002
http://www.capstone-press.com

Library of Congress Cataloging-in-Publication Data
Gibson, Karen Bush.
  Mississippi facts and symbols/by Karen Bush Gibson.
  p. cm.—(The states and their symbols)
  Includes bibliographical references and index.
  Summary: Presents information about the state of Mississippi, its nickname, motto,
and emblems.
  ISBN 0-7368-0640-7
  1. Emblems, State—Mississippi—Juvenile literature. [1. Emblems, State—Mississippi.
2. Mississippi.] I. Title. II. Series.
CR203.M7 G53 2001
976.2—dc21   00-022920

Editorial Credits
Sarah L. Schuette, editor; Linda Clavel, production designer and illustrator;
  Heidi Schoof and Kimberly Danger, photo researchers

Photo Credits
James P. Rowan, 6
KAC Productions/Bill Draker, 12; Kathy Adams Clark, 16
Leonard Lee Rue, Jr./FPG International LLC, cover
Mississippi Department of Archives and History, 22 (top)
Mississippi Department of Economic and Community Development, 22 (middle)
One Mile Up, Inc., 8, 10 (inset)
Root Resources/Dennis McDonald, 10; Alan G. Nelson, 18
Visuals Unlimited/H. A. Miller, 14; Gary Robinson, 20;
  Andrew J. Cunningham, 22 (bottom)

2 3 4 5 6 06 05 04 03 02 01

Table of Contents

Tennessee

Arkansas

Mississippi River

MISSISSIPPI

Alabama

Louisiana

Vicksburg National
Military Park

🏛

⭐ Jackson

Grand Village
of the Natchez Indians
🏛

● Natchez

Biloxi ●
🏛
Gulf Islands
National Seashore

✪	Capital
○	City
🏛	Places to Visit
〰	River

Gulf of Mexico

Fast Facts

Capital: Jackson is the capital of Mississippi.

Largest City: Jackson is the largest city in Mississippi. About 200,000 people live in Jackson.

Size: Mississippi covers 47,689 square miles (123,515 square kilometers). It is the 31st largest state.

Location: Mississippi is located in the southeastern United States.

Population: 2,768,619 people live in Mississippi (U.S. Census Bureau, 1999 estimate).

Statehood: On December 10, 1817, Mississippi became the 20th state to join the United States.

Natural Resources: Mississippi's natural resources include lumber, petroleum, and natural gas.

Manufactured Goods: Mississippi businesses make paper products, processed foods, and chemicals. They also build ships.

Crops: Mississippi farmers grow cotton, peanuts, rice, sugar cane, and soybeans. Livestock farmers raise cattle, hogs, and poultry. Mississippi also is the world's leading producer of pond-raised catfish.

State Name and Nickname

Mississippi's name comes from the Mississippi River. The Mississippi River forms the western border of the state. Mississippi is a Native American word that comes from the Chippewa and Algonquin languages. The name means "father of waters" and "great river." The Mississippi River is a large river that is fed by many smaller rivers.

Mississippi's nickname is the Magnolia State. The magnolia is the state flower and tree. Many magnolia trees grow in Mississippi.

Some people call Mississippi the Mud-Cat State. Mud-cat is another word for catfish. Mississippi farmers raise catfish in ponds. Many people like to eat catfish.

Another nickname for Mississippi is the Eagle State. The eagle appears on Mississippi's state seal. Eagles represent strength.

In 1541, Hernando de Soto became the first European to see the Mississippi River.

State Seal and Motto

Mississippi's government adopted its state seal in 1817. The seal represents Mississippi's government. It also makes state government papers official.

The Mississippi state seal looks like the U.S. seal. An eagle appears in the middle of the seal. The eagle is holding an olive branch in one claw. Olive branches represent peace. Arrows are in the eagle's other claw. The arrows stand for war. A shield with a U.S. flag design is on the front of the eagle.

Mississippi's state motto is "Virtue et Armis." These Latin words mean "by valor and arms." Valor means courage. Arms means strength. In 1894, James Rhea Preston, the Mississippi superintendent of education, suggested this motto.

Mississippi's state seal features an eagle in the center. The eagle stands for strength.

State Capitol and Flag

Jackson is the capital of Mississippi. Mississippi's capitol building is in Jackson. Government officials meet there to make the state's laws.

Jackson has had two capitol buildings. The first building was the capitol from 1839 to 1903. Today, the building is called the Old Capitol Museum. Visitors learn about Mississippi's history at the museum.

Workers built the second capitol in 1903. The capitol is made of gray sandstone and marble. A dome and a lamp are on top of the building. A golden eagle sits on the lamp.

Mississippi adopted its state flag in 1894. The flag has horizontal stripes of blue, white, and red. A Confederate flag is in the upper left corner of the flag. This small flag shows two blue bars crossed on a red background. Stars in the middle of these bars stand for the first 13 states to join the United States.

Theodore Link designed Mississippi's capitol to look like the U.S. Capitol in Washington, D.C.

State Bird

The mockingbird became Mississippi's state bird in 1944. The Women's Federated Club of Mississippi voted for the mockingbird. Mockingbirds are native to the United States and Mexico.

Mockingbirds are gray with white patches on their wings. They grow to be about 11 inches (28 centimeters) long. Mockingbirds have long tails.

The male mockingbird builds the nest for the female. Mockingbird nests sit on low branches of trees. The female lays three to five small eggs in the spring. Mockingbird eggs are blue and green with brown spots.

Mockingbirds copy, or mock, the sounds and songs of other birds. Scientists have found that some mockingbirds can sing like 36 other kinds of birds. Mockingbirds can even copy the sounds of other animals.

Mockingbirds eat insects, fruit, and seeds.

State Tree

Mississippi adopted the magnolia as the state tree in 1938. Mississippi schoolchildren voted for the state tree. Magnolia trees grow in the southeastern United States.

Magnolias are evergreen trees. Evergreen trees keep their leaves all year. Magnolias have straight trunks and many branches. The magnolia tree grows to be 100 feet (30 meters) tall.

The magnolia tree has large oval-shaped leaves. The leaves are 10 inches (25 centimeters) long. Magnolia leaves are dark green and have a waxy coating. This coating protects the leaves in winter.

In May, the magnolia tree blooms. Large white blooms grow on the branches in summer. The magnolia bloom is the state flower.

The magnolia tree grows best in warm, moist places such as Mississippi.

State Flower

The magnolia bloom became Mississippi's state flower in 1952. Mississippi officials voted for the state flower. The magnolia bloom grows on Mississippi's state tree.

The magnolia is named after French scientist Pierre Magnol. Magnol was a famous botanist who studied plants and trees in the 1600s.

Magnolia blooms grow as wide as 12 inches (30 centimeters). The flowers have six or more white petals. They are cup-shaped and smell like lemons.

Small red seeds fall from the middle of the bloom in autumn. Seeds from the magnolia bloom help to make more flowers. Bees drink nectar from the magnolia bloom. The bees use nectar to make honey.

Magnolia blooms smell like lemons.

State Land Mammals

The white-tailed deer became Mississippi's state land mammal in 1974. White-tailed deer live in wooded areas of the United States. They eat weeds, nuts, shrubs, and mushrooms that grow in Mississippi's forests.

Male deer have antlers. The male is called a buck. Every winter bucks lose their antlers. The female deer is called a doe. The doe does not have antlers.

Mississippi government officials adopted the red fox as the second official land mammal in 1997. Red foxes have pointed ears, red fur, and a long white-tipped tail. Their bodies grow to be 42 inches (107 centimeters) long. The red fox eats mice, rabbits, birds, and fruit.

The female red fox gives birth to as many as ten cubs in the summer. Both the male and the female fox care for the cubs.

White-tailed deer live in the wooded areas of Mississippi.

State Fossil: Mississippi adopted the prehistoric whale as the state fossil in 1981. Scientists found a complete skeleton of a prehistoric whale in Mississippi in 1971.

State Insect: The honeybee became Mississippi's state insect in 1980. Honeybees are social insects. As many as 80,000 bees live together in one hive.

State Stone: Mississippi named petrified wood the state stone in 1976. The Mississippi Petrified Forest has giant trees that are up to 36 million years old.

State Waterfowl: The wood duck became Mississippi's state waterfowl in 1974. Wood ducks live near forests and streams. Many wood ducks swim along the Mississippi River.

State Water Mammal: Mississippi named the bottle-nosed dolphin the state water mammal in 1974. Dolphins live in groups called pods.

Bottle-nosed dolphins swim along the Mississippi coastline.

Places to Visit

Grand Village of the Natchez Indians

Visitors to the Grand Village of the Natchez Indians near Natchez, Mississippi, explore Natchez history and culture. They participate in storytelling, living history programs, and the annual Natchez powwow.

Gulf Islands National Seashore

The Gulf Islands National Seashore is in southern Mississippi. About 26 miles (41 kilometers) of white sand beaches stretch along this area. Visitors swim, sail, and scuba dive. Many people visit the barrier islands and the Biloxi historic lighthouse.

Vicksburg National Military Park

The Vicksburg National Military Park gives visitors the chance to learn Civil War history. Soldiers fought more than 300 battles in Mississippi during the Civil War. Visitors tour the battlefields and a museum. They also look at Civil War artifacts such as cannons and uniforms.

Words to Know

artifact (ART-uh-fakt)—an object made by human beings, especially a tool or weapon used in the past

botanist (BOT-uh-nist)—a scientist who studies plants

mammal (MAM-uhl)—a warm-blooded animal with a backbone

petrified wood (PET-ri-fyed WOOD)—wood that turns into stone

powwow (POW-wow)—a social gathering for Native Americans featuring traditional dances and music

prehistoric whale (pree-hi-STOR-ik WALE)—a large ocean mammal that lived millions of years ago

skeleton (SKEL-uh-tuhn)—the bones that support and protect the body

superintendent (soo-pur-in-TEN-duhnt)—a person in charge of a building or a school

Read More

Hamill, Annette. *Hooray for Mississippi!: A Child's Journey into the History and Culture of Mississippi.* Brandon, Miss.: Quail Ridge Press, 1996.

Kummer, Patricia K. *Mississippi.* One Nation. Mankato, Minn.: Capstone Books, 1999.

Shirley, David. *Mississippi.* Celebrate the States. New York: Benchmark Books, 1999.

Useful Addresses

**Department of Economic
    Development**
P.O. Box 849
Jackson, MS 39205-0849

**Mississippi Gulf Coast
    Visitors Bureau**
P.O. Box 6128
Gulfport, MS 39506-6128

Internet Sites

Facts about Mississippi
http://www.maris.state.ms.us/htms/msfacts.htm

Mississippi Tourism
http://www.visitmississippi.org

State of Mississippi
http://www.state.ms.us

Index